I recommend PASS, SET, CRUSH to anyone associated with volleyball. The skills are shown and explained exactly. I give it a top rating.

Tom Selleck
Twice U.S. National Champion, 35 and Over

I wish I had had the visual reference provided by PASS, SET, CRUSH when I was giving clinics. Everyone—from junior high kids to adults—would have benefited.

Jeff Reddan, Player/Coach
Seattle Smashers, Professional League
Four-time Professional All-Star

PASS, SET, CRUSH is the definitive study of volleyball techniques.

Taras Liskevych, Head Coach
USA Women's Volleyball Team
Olympic Qualifiers, 1988

Lucas has taken the "umbrella" approach: he covers in detail the methods that work best in performing volleyball skills. Focus on these and become a better player.

Aldis Berzins
Olympic Gold Medal, 1984
World Cup Champion, 1985

Jeff Lucas' PASS, SET, CRUSH is a well-thought-out, valuable addition to the volleyball enthusiast's library.

Bill Neville
USVBA Technique Director
Olympic Gold Medal, 1984

PASS, SET, CRUSH is a solid work. Any student of the game will find it worth reading.

Chuck Erbe, Head Coach
USC Women's Volleyball Team
Winner of 4 collegiate National Championships
Winner of 3 USVBA National Championships

> First volleyball book in 25 years to be translated from English into Japanese.

PASS, SET, CRUSH

VOLLEYBALL ILLUSTRATED

Second Edition

by Jeff Lucas

ILLUSTRATED BY STUART MOLDREM

EUCLID NORTHWEST PUBLICATIONS
Wenatchee, Washington

Library of Congress Cataloging-in-Publication Data

Lucas, Jeff, 1946-
　　Pass, set, crush.

　　Bibliography: p.
　　Includes index.
　　1. Volleyball.　I. Moldrem, Stuart.　II. Title.
GV1015.3.L83　1988　　　796.32′5　　　88-3636
ISBN 0-9615088-2-5
ISBN 0-9615088-3-3 (pbk.)

Second Edition
1988

Published by Euclid Northwest Publications
　　　　4227 Crestview Street
　　　　Wenatchee, WA 98801

ISBN 0-9615088-3-3 (Softcover)
ISBN 0-9615088-2-5 (Hardcover)

Chapter III drawings from photos by J.B. Saunders
Page 157 drawing from photo by Diane Williams

CONTENTS

For Wenatchee High Volleyball players
who were great teachers

Acknowledgments

I am indebted to the following for their help:

Jim Holcomb, who founded the Wenatchee Volleyball Club and offered me my first coaching job

Marilyn Stewart, Bob Eller, Tom Byrne and all those in the Wenatchee School District who gave me the opportunity to coach at Wenatchee High School

Shelly Field, who did much of the photography

Stuart Moldrem, artist *extraordinaire*

Merle and Anne Dowd, who directed the production of the book

Hartwig Petersen who patiently assembled the mechanicals

Doug Beal, who supported my using Dave Saunders as a demonstrator

Tom Tait, who read the manuscript and offered seven hours' worth of suggestions, many of which became a part of the book

Jürgen Sabarz, for the use of his photo

Kit's Cameras of Wenatchee and Price Photo of Seattle

The players and coaches of the U.S. National teams

The U.S. Volleyball Association, the Evergreen Region and especially the members of the Wenatchee Volleyball Club for giving me an opportunity to play

INTRODUCTION

The writer of an athletic technique book is confronted with a dilemma. If the book is to be helpful, it must say, "This is the way to do it." Yet the writer knows that the descriptions cannot be absolutely perfect for everyone; body builds make a difference. The solution, it seems to me, lies in quantity. What if the writer could bring the reader very near to perfect—say, about 95 percent of the way? Or, to use an analogy: what if the book could illuminate a *target* called "perfect technique," even though the exact location of its bull's-eye were to remain unknown?

My intention is to illuminate the target "perfect technique." To this end, I have devoted parts of 10 years, shot 7,000 photos, studied 52 books on volleyball, attended numerous clinics and camps, talked to the best players and coaches in the world and hit thousands of balls.

The technical basis for this book is provided by the performances of the best players in the world. It is they—not the coaches—who advance volleyball's knowledge of individual skills. Their bodies, through repetition, simply find the easiest or most effective ways to perform.

* * * * *

The most striking thing about volleyball skills is the importance of the body's center of gravity. In three of the five most important skills, the center of gravity (in the area of the hips) holds the key to either balance or power. Pushing the hips back keeps the forearm passer on balance; snapping them forward gives power to the spiker; and rotating them makes the Asian serve more powerful than the overhand.

The demonstrators include: Dave Saunders of the United States Men's volleyball team, winner of the Olympic gold medal in 1984, the World Cup in 1985, and the World Championship in 1986 (spike, block); Steve Suttich, former U.C.L.A. All-American and former head volleyball coach at the University of Washington (dig); Debbie Green of the United States Women's team, winner of the Olympic silver medal in 1984, and First Team Professional All-Star in 1987 (setter's tip); Shelly Field, formerly Whitman College Volleyball (forearm pass, roll); Cathy Kuntz, Portland State University Volleyball, 1985-86 National Champion (set, collapse); Kari Becker, Eastern Washington University Volleyball (other attacks); and Jeff Lucas, Wenatchee Volleyball Club (serve, dive).

The demonstrators were chosen because they were able to show the skills easily. There was no intent to choose a male for this skill or a female for that. All of the skills work equally well for either sex.

The illustrations—pencil on coquille board—were drawn by Stuart Moldrem, professional painter and sports illustrator for the *Seattle Post Intelligencer* for 35 years. Many of the illustrations are sequences; all of these are arranged from left to right. The demonstrators are all right-handed. The left-hander simply needs to reverse the images and substitute "left" for "right" and vice versa.

The book assumes that the reader knows the way volleyball is played; for example, that the object of the game is to put the ball on the opponents' floor, that each team is allowed three contacts of the ball, that serves are usually received on the forearms, etc. Having seen a match should give the reader enough knowledge to follow the book.

The first three chapters cover the contacts in a typical offensive play in order: the pass, the set and the attack. This arrangement also corresponds, not coincidentally, to the book's title. The following chapters and sections are ordered roughly by the importance of the skills covered.

CHAPTER I
THE PASS

The forearm pass is a method of bouncing the ball from both forearms (**1**). The combination of ball and forearms makes the skill unique in North American sports. It is primarily used in serve-receive and, thus, starts the team's offense.

1

In its short history experts have asked one main question about the forearm pass: How can the passer move quickly into a hard serve and still make a soft pass? For many years leg straightening was thought to be the secret (2). But leg straightening is slow. This means that the player must start her passing motion early. She must commit herself to the ball while it is still a distance away. Last moment adjustments are difficult for her.

2a   b

The present-day passer uses a short armswing (**3**). Her legs do not move during the pass, nor does any part of her body (except her arms). Arms are quicker than legs. With an armswing, the passer can wait until the last moment to start her passing motion. She is like the baseball batter with "quick wrists"; she does not need to swing until she has the best possible idea where the ball is going.

There is a further advantage to the armswing pass. Since the passer's whole body is still, including her head and eyes, she can watch the ball more closely. The passer slows or stops her forearms to make a soft pass.

3

4

Ready

A good ready position is high and relaxed (4). A bent or low position is tiring and hurts a quick start. A good ready position is also compact. The passer keeps her hands on or near her body. Her feet are side-by-side and spread, but not too much. She bends her knees slightly.

Balance is all-important. The passer who has perfect balance when the ball is served gets a quick and controlled start. Weight held on the front part of the feet (so that the passer can push with her toes) helps balance. So does positioning the hips slightly to the rear. A slight shifting of the weight from side-to-side, or a slight sway of the upper body, or a slight up-and-down movement also helps.

Getting to the Ball

The Foot Position

The player wants to pass with a foot position that brings, above all, stability. The best passers in the world have found that the most solid is like the police officer's in shooting a pistol: side-by-side, flat on the floor and wide (**5**). Pointing the toes and knees slightly inward, which locks the hips, makes the position even more stable.

The stride position—one foot in front of the other—allows only the front foot to be flat on the floor; it is not as solid as the side-by-side.

5

The passer's first job, once she sees the ball coming to her, is to move her feet to the ball (6). Once arrived, she will position them side-by-side, as mentioned. Feet go before arms. Sometimes it seems natural for the passer's arms to reach toward the ball first. The player then ends up going to the passing spot with her arms held out (7). This is a mistake. Arms held out slow the passer's movement to the ball.

Three more points:

1. The passer watches the ball all during her movement to the passing spot.
2. She carries most of her weight on the front part of her feet.
3. She lowers her body slightly for better balance.

7

6

8

The Bounce

When the ball is going to arrive nearby, the passer makes a series of quick bounces to adjust her position (8). She keeps her feet side-by-side and holds her arms comfortably away from her body for balance. The front part of her feet does the springing.

The Side-Step

The bounce turns into a side-step when the passer moves to her side (**9**). She leads with the foot nearer the passing site and follows with a skip-step (**a, b**). The passer completes the movement with her feet in the side-by-side position, ready either to pass or to make another side-step (**c**).

Both bouncing and side-stepping allow the passer to face the serve as she moves and also to stop easily.

9a

b

c

9

The Cross-and-Run

When the ball is served more than two or three steps away, the passer needs to cross-and-run (**10**). She leads with the foot nearer the passing site, as in the side-step, but begins to turn her foot and her body toward the ball (**b**).

10a

b

The passer's second step makes the cross (**c**). It completes her turn away from the server; her hips have rotated 90 degrees. Her toes point to the side.

The cross helps the passer to speed up. She can run for the ball once she is turned. Running is faster than side-stepping. However, running makes stopping more difficult.

c

11a   b

The Hop

In order to stop from a run, the passer needs to hop (**11**). The hop turns her body back toward the server and places her feet in the side-by-side position (**c**).

The player also needs to hop after moving forward. This can be difficult, especially when the serve is very short. For an extremely short serve, it is smoother to make the pass with one foot in front of the other. This is also the case for a high serve or a free ball.

Most serve-receive formations do not require the passer to move backward more than a step. A bounce or two brings her into position in this case.

In order to get to the ball, the forearm passer:

1. Moves her feet first
2. Hops into passing position
3. Places her feet
   a. side-by-side
   b. wider than her shoulders
   c. flat on the floor

c

12

The Pass

The best way for the passer to join her hands is by interlocking her fingers at the first knuckle (**12, 13**). She relies on the heels of her hands— they are pressed together—to square her forearms. Unlike other grips, inter- locking fingers leaves the forearm muscles relaxed. This means that the passer can move her arms at their quickest. Relaxed forearm muscles bring the greatest gains in quickness when the passer reaches to the side (**13**).

13

Once the passer has a good hand clasp, she needs to position her forearms. There are three things that help make her passes accurate:

1. The passer locks her elbows so that her arms do not bend. This allows her arms to work as one.

2. She rolls her forearms outward, turning the flat part of her forearms toward the ball.

3. She holds her forearms as close together as possible, making double hits less likely (**12, 13**).

14

A good body position is low for balance (**14**). The passer bends her knees and pushes her upper body forward at the waist. She straightens her back by pushing her hips to the rear. Hips pushed back are all-important in keeping the passer balanced: she is solid from the beginning to the end of her pass.

Hips held forward round the passer's back (**15**). This means that her head and shoulders are too far back for balance. The passer with a rounded back falls backward during or after the pass.

The only time the passer draws her hips forward is in handling topspin: digging a hard spike or receiving a topspin serve (**16**). Her arms need to be nearly vertical to keep the topspinning ball from climbing straight up or, worse yet, jumping backward. Hips held forward balance her arms in their nearly vertical position.

15

16

17

The arms swing from the shoulders to meet the ball (**17**). The armswing is short: the hands move only a few inches and then stop at about 45 degrees to the floor. This is the best arm angle for passing most serves. The player may swing *through* a slow, easy ball. But swinging through a hard serve usually results in a high or hard pass. These passes are difficult to set. When the serve is coming very fast, the passer waits until the last moment to start her armswing. She tries to watch the serve as long as possible.* Then she must move her arms quickly forward and, in order not to hit the ball too hard, pull them back just after contact. The ball touches the forearms one third to one half the distance from wrist to elbow.

Here are the main points for the forearm pass. The player:

1. Presses the heels of her hands together
2. Locks her elbows
3. Rolls her arms out and holds them near each other
4. Bends her knees and her waist
5. Pushes her hips to the rear
6. Holds her body and her head still
7. Uses a short armswing, stopping near 45 degrees
8. Touches the ball 3 or 4 inches above her wrists

*The passer does not "look the ball into her forearms." Tilting her head forward or looking suddenly downward interferes with her vision. She simply watches the ball as long as she can without making quick head or eye movements.

CHAPTER II
THE SET

18

The set or overhand pass is a method of pushing the ball upward with both hands (**18**). It is the most accurate pass in volleyball and the main tool of its magicians, the setters.

The best setters contact the ball near their foreheads. They stay in contact with the ball as it moves toward the target. They continue to touch it until their arms are straight. These setters have a soft, but commanding "touch." A soft but commanding touch is the result of two things: wrists that spring (soft) and arms that squeeze (commanding).

19

20

Getting to the Ball

As in forearm passing, the setter must first move her feet to the ball (19). She can either side-step or run. She will never move backward if she can help it. There is too great a chance to be whistled for holding. The player arrives facing the target, with the ball directed toward her forehead (20). Her shoulders are square—at a 90 degree angle with a line drawn to the target. From this position both arms can push in the same way.

Ready to Pass

The Feet

There are two positions for the feet: *stride* and *side-by-side*. The stride position is like a short walking step (**21**)*. The feet are shoulder width apart. The front foot is flat on the floor; the heel of the rear foot is raised. In the side-by-side position both feet are in a line 90 degrees to the target (**22**). They are close to each other—only a few inches apart—and flat on the floor. The toes point toward the target.

*Invariably the setter positions her right foot forward. This allows her to turn easily from left to right, from facing her teammates as they pass to facing down the net as she sets. In most of the illustrations (Fig. 21, for example), the setter's *left* foot is forward. The reason for this is to keep the left-to-right format of the illustrations and still show both legs of the setter.

23a b

The stride position is used almost all the time. When the setter is standing, she steps forward into the stride, shifting most of her weight to her front foot (**23a, b**). She bends her knees slightly, and then straightens her legs as she pushes the ball upward (**b, c**). Leg straightening adds force to the set.

c   24

When the setter is running, her last step takes her into the stride (24). In this case the stride helps her to slow down. As in a standing start, her front leg carries most of her weight.

The setter almost always uses the stride. She needs balance as she steps or runs to the ball.

The side-by-side foot position gives extra power (25). Both the player's feet are under her weight instead of mainly the front one (a). Her legs are near to each other throughout their length, working in exactly the same way. They push forcefully as one (b).

The side-by-side setter tilts her body toward the target during the pass for the greatest power (a, b).

The side-by-side foot position is limited to players who do not need to chase the ball. These are usually not setters, but spikers playing the back row. They need to make a long set, but do not need the balance or stopping power of the stride.

25a   b

The Body

The setter bends her knees before making the pass, as mentioned. This gives her legs a chance to push. But there is one time when the setter will want to push with her legs very little: when she is in position to set two or more hitters (**26**). In this case she wants her body to be nearly motionless so that she can fool the blockers about where she intends to set. Her body is upright as she receives the ball; she waits as long as possible before starting her setting motion.

The setter tilts her head upward, watching the ball (**26**). Her back is straight and vertical. She holds her hands about 6 inches in front of her forehead while she waits for the ball. She does not move her head; her eyes follow the ball to her hands.

The set or overhand pass "ready" position is now complete. The setter has:

1. Moved her feet to the ball
2. Directed the ball toward her forehead
3. Faced the target
4. Positioned her feet in stride
5. Bent her knees
6. Tilted her head upward
7. Positioned her hands about 6 inches in front of her forehead

26

27a   b

The Pass

The Arms

The arms do only one thing in the set: they push the hands (**27**). The push, however, is important; it gives the setter a solid contact of the ball, a commanding touch. The setter's arms push her hands *inward* as well as forward (**27a, b**). This allows her to squeeze the ball, keeping it from straying to the left or right.

The setter's elbows are held very wide at ready (**27a**). Wide elbows put her arms in a plane, making for a direct squeeze (**28**). Wide elbows also position the passer's wrists for the greatest flex (to be discussed).

29a

b

At the start of the pass, the setter's forearms move toward the ball like arrows (**29a, b**). Her hand is the tip of the arrow; her elbow is the tail. This means that her hands and arms travel at an inward angle—about 45 degrees—until clamping the ball. Each hand touches the *side* of the ball (**29b**).

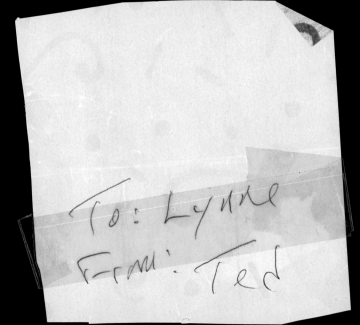

30a   **b**

Once the setter's hands are firmly touching the sides of the ball, they change direction. First, they were moving toward each other; now they move toward the target, straight forward (**30a, b**). The ball's resistance—not the player's effort—brings this change of direction.

31a   b

The setter continues to squeeze the ball as her hands and the ball move forward (**31**). Her elbows do not rotate or twist; they stay in a plane throughout the pass. Her hands are driven from a few inches in front of her forehead to full arm extension (**d**).

Should the setter pull her arms back as the ball arrives? No. A simple inward push works better. There are three reasons for this:

1. Pulling back must be timed with the ball's speed. Each ball arrives at

c   d

a different speed, and some are spinning. It is impossible be in time with every one.

2. Pulling back is slow. It takes extra time to pull back and then to push. This is important to the setter. She wants to pass quickly so that opposing blockers have little time to move into position. Also, the hitters time their approaches by the setting motion. A quick motion means fewer timing errors between the hitter and the setter.

3. Pulling back causes referees to sit up and take notice. The touch time is very long, so referees call fouls more strictly.

32a   b

The Wrists

A soft touch on the set can seem like magic to those who do not have it. But a soft touch only means that the ball changes direction in the player's hands *gradually* (**32**). Her wrists and, to a lesser extent, her fingers do the work.

The setter's wrists work as springs. In other words, they flex when the ball pushes on them (**b, c**). The setter does not need to think about the flex; the action is automatic. She does need to hold her hands gently back, without stiffness in either her hands or wrists (**a**). This is important, since every beginning player wants to tense the muscles of her hands and wrists toward the ball. Wrists held rigid do not flex.

33   34

There is one more thing the player does to gain wrist flexibility and a soft touch. She positions her wrists so that the ball pushes them squarely back (**33**). "Squarely back" means that the arriving ball tilts her hand neither toward her thumb nor her little finger. Wide elbows, both at ready and during the pass, keep the player's wrists square as the ball pushes on them (**33, 34, 35, 36**).

35

36a   b

37a　　　　b

38　　　　39

The Hands

Once the setter's elbows are wide and her wrists square, she needs to open her hands to receive the ball. "Open" is important. The player holds the fingertips of one hand together and then opens her fingers gently; this motion gives her the hand position she wants at contact with the ball (**37a, b**). Her hands are cupped, her fingers slightly curled (**38, 39, 40, 41, 42**). There is firmness, but it comes from opening her fingers, not from tensing them forward. Tensed fingers do not flex.

The setter holds her hands about 6 inches in front of her forehead (**40, 41, 42**). The left is held exactly like the right (**39**). Her index fingers are nearly in a line and about 8 inches apart — wider than they will be on the ball (**38, 39**).

40

41

42

43 a   b   c   d

The Entire Motion

The player intending to set or overhand pass raises her hands early — as soon as she knows the ball is coming to her (**43a**). She starts moving her arms early, too, well before the ball touches her hands (**b**).

Once the setter has started moving her arms toward the ball, she must put up her biggest fight. The muscles of her arms are working, pushing her hands toward the ball. But the muscles of her hands are not. The setter must hold her hands gently but firmly back.

The problem becomes acute just before and during the player's touch of the ball (**c**). Her hands want to *do* something to the ball. They cannot. They must let the ball act on them. The doing is in the arms.

The ball first touches the pads of the fingers, on the fingerprint. It pushes the fingers back, spreading them about the ball (**d**). The ball sinks deep into the setter's hands, finally touched by the length of her fingers and the pads of her thumbs. The setter's wrists are also pushed back by the force of the ball. This is the important instant: hands and wrists are flexing automatically — backward — as the arms move forward.

e   f   g   h

By this time the ball has stopped moving toward the player and is about to reverse its direction and head for the target. This is the moment that the setter puts the greatest pressure on the ball. Her hands, on each side of the ball and pushed by her arms, squeeze it firmly.

Now the ball is moving away from the player (**e**). The setter's hands and wrists rebound so that they stay in contact with the ball as it moves away. Pressure on the ball is still inward, though less and less so (**f**).

The setter continues to touch the ball until her arms are nearly straight (**g**). The last contact is made with the tips of the fingers.

Since the player has avoided tightening her wrists during the pass, her hands turn outward as the ball leaves (**h**). The player's arms are straight and parallel at the end of the motion, about a ball's width apart (**44**). The ball leaves cleanly and without spin.

When the arriving ball is high or spinning, the setter needs greater resistance. She must start her hands toward the ball sooner, giving them greater speed at contact. She must also firm her hands and wrists. Both of these changes help to keep the ball from breaking through her hands. They also decrease the setter's spring of the ball, which does not sink so deeply into her hands.

44

44

The Back Set

The setter can pass the ball to a teammate behind her, that is, to back-set (**46**). She receives the ball in exactly the same position as in setting forward (**a**). She contacts the ball in the same place—in front of her forehead (**b**). She springs and squeezes the ball as in front setting, but for the back-set quickly pushes it over her head (**c**). Her shoulders move backward with her arms; her hips move forward. As in front setting, she stays in contact with the ball as long as possible.

The Jump Set

The setter can combine her overhand pass with a jump (**45**). There are three times when she will want to do this:

1. The pass from her teammate is high and long. She jumps to keep from touching the net.

2. She wants to quicken her attack. She jumps in order to set the ball sooner, before it falls.

3. She is in the front row and likes to attack the second touch. She jumps so that her opponents do not know what she will do — attack or set.

Jumping brings two differences to the set:

1. There is a delay between the leg push (jump) and the pass itself. This means that the rhythm is different than in setting from the floor: "jump," then "set." The entire motion takes more time.

2. The setter has less power in midair. She cannot push with her legs as she can on the floor.

45

I. Here are the main points of the set or overhand pass. The player gets ready to receive the ball by:

1. Moving her feet to the ball
2. Positioning her forehead in the ball's path
3. Facing the target
4. Positioning her feet in stride
5. Bending her knees
6. Tilting her head upward
7. Positioning her elbows wide
8. Holding her hands
   a. back
   b. open
   c. 6 inches in front of her forehead
   d. nearly horizontal (index fingers point slightly upward)

II. Once the player is ready, she:

1. Starts her arms before the ball arrives
2. Pushes her arms inward
3. Touches the sides of the ball
4. Allows the ball to spread her hands and flex her wrists
5. Straightens her arms to full extension
6. Stays in contact with the ball as long as possible
7. Straightens her legs as her arms push the ball outward

47

CHAPTER III
THE SPIKE

The spike is a method of smashing the ball into the opponents' court (**47**). There is no other athletic skill—in any sport—quite like it. Why? Because the player must hit the ball as hard as he can *while in midair*. He can't push on the floor for power, as in throwing. This means he must use his body in a special way: against itself.

The player uses his body "against itself" both by bending and twisting in midair (**47**). His lower body—especially his hips—makes the base against which he does this. The position of the player's hips is most important in developing power in midair.

48

To Pike or Not to Pike

"To pike" means to bend forward at the waist. Piking is common among spikers (**48**). In fact, a good pike has been thought to show that the hitter has smashed the ball with all his power. Quite the opposite is true. The pike represents power that was not given to the ball.

Newton's third law of motion says that for every action there is an equal and opposite reaction. Applied to the spike, this might read: The harder the spiker hits the ball, the more his body stops at contact.* Said in another way, the spiker whose body stops cold at contact has hit with power (**49**). The hitter who pikes has not.

How does the spiker avoid piking? Or, how does he generate enough power that contact stops his body cold?

1. The spiker must time perfectly the motions of his body, hitting arm and hand. They move in a sequence, like the uncoiling of a whip.

2. The spiker must hit the ball when his body is perfectly straight.*

Hitting the ball with a perfectly straight body is important in developing power. It is also difficult to do. The secret is in the spiker's hips: they must snap quickly forward during the jump. The hitter whose hips have not snapped forward during the jump has no chance to bring them forward once he is in the air. What snaps the hips forward? The spiker's body position *before* he starts his jump is most important. He must time his armswing well. Also, he must draw his hips back. He must cock them. Hips that have been cocked can snap forward during the jump. A timely armswing and a cocking of the hips are the keys to power in the spike.

*For further explanation, see the Appendix to Chapter III.

49a   b

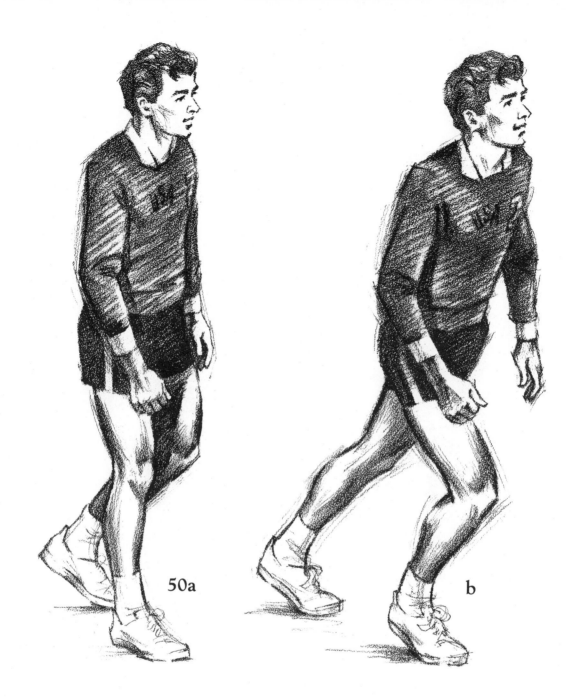

50a

b

Getting to the Ball

Ready

The ready position for the spike is like the distance runner's: one foot leads the other (**a**). There is one big difference, however. The spiker holds all his weight on his front foot, allowing him to start upright; the runner distributes his weight more evenly, leaning forward at the start. The right-handed spiker positions his right foot forward.

The right-hander wants to contact the ball slightly in front of his right shoulder. His run brings him into position to do this.

c

d

The Steps

The spiker makes a four-, three- or two-step run to the ball. The four-step is standard and easiest to learn. Players who need to be quicker simply drop one or both of the first two steps (at a loss of speed in the run).

The right-handed spiker starts his four-step run with a quick step to the rear using his left foot (**a, b**). It is as if he is stepping forward with his right foot—though his right does not leave the floor. This quick step backward allows him to start nearer the point of his attack, but still gives him a "step" with his right for extra speed. His right foot is counted as Step 1 of the four-step approach (**b**).*

Step 2, taken with the left foot by the right-handed spiker, is longer than Step 1 (**c, d**). The spiker increases his speed during Step 2.

*The spiker who is already moving takes a full step with his right foot in the course of his run.

49

51a   b

Step 3, taken with the right foot, is long and quick (**a, b**). It speeds up the approach. Step 4 brings the spiker's left foot into position next to his right for the jump (**c, d**). It is also quick. The player can count evenly "one-two-three" during his four-step approach. The last two steps—one after the other—occur in the time it takes to say "three."

COUNT	STEPS
1	right
2	left
3	right/left

Steps 3 and 4 put the player's feet side-by-side. His toes point about 45 degrees to the right of the target (**d**). His body, too, has turned to the right, toward his hitting hand. The turn is important. The spiker wants to position his hips in the air at this 45 degree angle.

52a
b

The Armswing

The armswing gives the spiker a higher jump. He throws his arms upward and his body follows. But the armswing plays an even bigger role in a successful spike. A well-timed armswing helps the spiker to bring his hips back on Step 3, so that he can snap them forward during his jump. The spiker then can hit the ball when his body is straight. He does not pike. The spiker gives all of his power to the ball.

Most spikers' armswings are late. Late means that the player does not have time to swing his arms fully forward and up. He must stop his armswing and quickly raise his arms to hit. Without a full armswing, it is difficult for the spiker to move his hips back and then forward. He pikes, losing power.

The timing of the armswing is determined early in the approach—during Step 3 (**a, b**). At this point the spiker's arms swing backward as his body speeds forward. Step 3 is where the hitter is likely to have trouble: his arms do not want to move in the direction

opposite to his body. The spiker allows his arms to swing as far to the rear as possible (**b**). His shoulders limit his armswing to the rear.

The spiker's arms stop their backswing just before his right foot hits the floor (**b**). This is an important point in timing the armswing and the steps.

The spiker's arms swing forward with power during Step 4. They move in a straight line, crossing the spiker's body near his hips (**c**). His arms are slightly forward of his hips as he starts his jump and horizontal in the middle of it (**d**). They swing above his head as he leaves the floor (**e**). His arms are nearly straight throughout their swing.

The forward and upward swing of the spiker's arms helps to tilt his upper body: his hips move forward and his shoulders back (**c, d, e**). This allows him to hit the ball when his body is straight, using all of his power.

53a   b

The Hips

The spiker's backward armswing starts the tilting of his upper body—bringing his hips back and his shoulders forward (**53a**). The spiker must now continue the motion, bending his body forward at the waist.

As the spiker starts his armswing forward, his hips continue to move to the rear (**b**). His shoulders dip toward his knees. He bends severely at the waist; his upper body and his thighs make a sharp angle. The spiker's back is arched, increasing the effect of his bend (**b**).

This is the most important moment in the spike. The spiker has coiled his body. His hips are cocked back, ready to snap forward. His shoulders are down, ready to drive upward and back. His back is arched. He is now in position to hit the ball with maximum power. His body will be perfectly straight at contact.

As the spiker's arms swing forward, his hips also move forward (**c, d, e**). His shoulders, on the other hand, start moving to the rear. His torso is nearly vertical during the upward thrust of his legs (**c, d**).

By the time the spiker has left the floor, his hips have snapped forward. They are set in the air (**e**).

54

c   d   e

The Foot Action

The spiker's hips move sharply forward as he jumps. His feet reflect the movement of his hips. They roll forward on the floor like rolling pins—heel to toe (**a, b, c, d**).

The spiker's right heel hits the floor first (**a**). His right toe quickly follows (**b**). His right heel leaves the floor, continuing its rolling action (**c**). Now his left foot joins in, touching down (**c**). By this time the spiker's hips have driven far enough forward that *only his left toe* touches the floor. His left heel never contacts the floor (**c**).

Now the toes of both feet roll forward together (**d**). The spiker continues the rolling action even as he leaves the floor (**e**). It is as if he is trying to keep his toes on the floor, pointing them downward as he jumps (**e**). This corresponds to the snap of his hips; they are now well ahead of his shoulders (**e**). He can now arch his back in the extreme without piking during his hit.

The player's feet hitting the floor can be counted evenly "heel, toe, toe." The spiker pushes equally hard with the toes of both feet, giving him a square jump.

54

55

The Jump

The spiker wants to jump so that his body is vertical in the air (**55**). Jumping with a forward lean means that he cannot reach as high; he contacts the ball lower (**54**). He may, however, fly forward during his jump (like the long jumper in track). A fast run brings a forward jump of from 1 to 3 feet—but with the body vertical. The spiker's feet and hips point in the same direction during the upward part of his jump—to the right of the target.

I. In order to time his run, the spiker:

    1. Lengthens and quickens Steps 3 and 4
    2. Swings his arms quickly backward during Step 3
    3. Finishes his arms' backswing just before Step 3 touches down
    4. Counts his four-step approach, 1-2-3

56a   b   c

II. In order to position his hips in the air, the spiker:

    1. Times his backward armswing to stop just before his right foot hits the floor
    2. Thrusts his hips backward, dips his shoulders and arches his back during Step 3 (**56a**)
    3. Points his feet (and his hips) 45 degrees to the right of the target on Steps 3 and 4 (**b**)
    4. Rolls his feet forward as he swings his arms (**b**)
    5. Pushes himself upward with the front part of his feet, heels raised
    6. Jumps with an equal push from the toes of both feet (**b**)
    7. Tilts his shoulders to the rear as he jumps
    8. Swings his arms well forward and above his head (**c**)

III. In order to jump high, the spiker:

    1. Swings his arms as far to the rear as possible (**a**)
    2. Times his arms so that they lead his body into the air (**b**)
    3. Keeps his body upright during his jump
    4. Swings both of his arms above his head (**c**)

57a   b

Cocking the Hammer

    The spiker's feet have left the floor; his hips are set in the air (**a**). He arches and twists his upper back (**b**). His left hand remains above his head, seeming to reach for the ball, as he arches and twists. His right arm draws back. The spiker bends his elbow to the extreme and moves it as far to the rear and as high as possible. This arm position is often called the "bow-and-arrow," for its similarity to archery.* His entire arm is held above his shoulder; his right hand is held palm-down and slightly out. Now the hitting motion, which is very similar to throwing, begins.

*The term "bow-and-arrow" is *approximate*. There are important differences between the spiker's arm position and the archer's: The spiker's right elbow is cocked well above the line of his shoulders (**b**). The archer's elbow stays in line with his shoulders. The spiker's left arm angles upward from his shoulder line (**b**). The archer's left arm lines up exactly with his shoulders.

The Hit

The spiker's body begins to straighten and to untwist (**c**). Now three things happen at once:

    1. His left arm moves downward toward his body
    2. His right hand drops back, sweeping above his ear (**c**)
    3. His right shoulder drives forward, leading his arm into the ball (**c**)

His elbow does not move ahead of the line of his shoulders. This is important. The spiker who pushes his elbow farther ahead is uncoiling his arm too early. The spiker's elbow remains high throughout his motion.

The spiker's arm unbends at the elbow as he turns into the ball. When his arm is straight—pointing upward—his wrist snaps (**d**). His hand contacts the ball directly over his right side and slightly in front of his shoulder. His fingers are spread. His body faces the target. The spiker's body is straight at contact (**d**). His hips and shoulders make a vertical line. His hand is moving at its fastest. He is solid in the air.

The Whip

   How does the spiker get power? By whipping his body. This means that he accumulates speed at its tip. The spiker's body can be seen as a series of four movable parts (**a**). His torso (heaviest) moves first (**b**). His upper arm moves next (**c**). His forearm follows (**d**). Finally the lightest part, his hand, moves into the ball (**e**).

c

d

e

Each part in turn *slows down* as its energy is transferred to the next part. His torso slows as his upper arm speeds up (**c**). His upper arm slows for his forearm (**d**), which in turn slows for his hand (**e**). These transfers accumulate great speed; his hand snaps like the tip of a towel or whip.

59

60

The player spikes the ball from as high as he can reach (**59**). This means that his hitting arm is nearly vertical at contact. How does he keep his arm nearly vertical and hit the ball down at different angles? By adjusting the location of his wrist snap (**60**). A change of an inch or two forward or back does not move his arm far from vertical. But it changes the angle of his hit a great deal.

61a　　　　　　　**b**

In order to hit the ball as hard as possible, the spiker:

1. Leaves his left arm pointing upward as his right draws back
2. Keeps his right elbow above his right shoulder during his draw-back and his hit (**61**)
3. Leads with his shoulder, elbow and wrist in order
4. Hits the ball as high as he can reach
5. Makes contact when his body is perfectly straight
6. Snaps his wrist over the ball
7. Spreads his fingers about the ball at contact
8. Faces the target both at contact and during his finish

d

b

c

The Finish

The spiker gives up a great deal of his energy to the ball at contact: his entire body either stops or slows down. His torso stops. Its final position is straight and vertical (**62**). His arm continues forward, but much more slowly. It finally stops near his side (**c**). This is his "follow-through" position. The spiker lands with his toes pointing directly toward the target.

63a   b

There is a final point about body rotation. The player jumps facing 45 degrees to the right of the target (**a**). He arches and twists; then he straightens. His torso develops its greatest power on return to its 45 degree position. But the spiker does not hit the ball facing to the right of the target. His body continues to rotate—past the 45 degrees—so that the spiker is facing the target when and after he hits (**b**). Why does his torso move past its position of greatest power? Because the whip does not end with his torso. It must go through his arm and hand. This takes the added time.

* * * * *

In the top row of the following sequence note the spiker's armswing, the backward and then forward movement of his hips and the tipping back of his shoulders. In the bottom row note the spiker's whip—the starting and stopping of his hips, the same for his shoulders and the stopping of his elbow before contact.

64

66

65a   b

*Note the turn of the spiker's hips (**a, b**), the rise of his elbow toward the ball (**c**), the severe tilt of his shoulders at contact (**d**), the rigidity of his whole body after the hit (**e**) and the straight-forward action of his arm on its follow-through (**e**).*

c   d   e

At the instant of touch
All is quiet.
The torso does not budge;
Neither do the legs,
Nor the head.
There is no resistance from the ball.
No pressure at the elbow,
No bump at the shoulder,
Not the slightest vibration
Anywhere in the body.
And no work.
Selected contractions,
Long since past,
Have done it all:
Hand speed
Beyond the imaginable,
Beyond control.
And the ball,
Astonished,
Makes a fast trip.

67

CHAPTER IV
THE SERVE

The serve is a method of throwing the ball and then hitting it over the net to start play (**67**). It is the only skill in volleyball in which the player has complete control of the ball. The server stands alone outside the court, waiting for a signal from the referee. His serving motion is slow. For these reasons, volleyball players usually have more mental problems with the serve than with any other skill.

The ball can be served so that it travels with or without spin.

68

Most spinning serves are hit with topspin (**68**). These curve downward in a smooth path. This means that the receiver of a spinner knows where it will go. To counteract the receiver's advantage, the server usually tries to serve very hard. But serving hard leads to mistakes. For this reason, intentional spinners are rare at all levels of competition. (The jump serve [page 107] is making the spinner less rare but no less risky.)

A spinless serve changes direction in midflight, dancing through the air (70). The ball's being out-of-round does the trick. A "hill" or high spot on the surface of the ball lowers the air pressure on that side. The ball is pulled toward the lower pressure as an airplane wing is drawn upward (69). The spinless ball moves to the left or right, up or down, depending on the location of its high spot. A slowly rotating ball curves to the left, then to the right, then back again to the left as its high spot turns from side to side (70).

(Placement of the valve stem has no influence on the ball's path. A ball made notably heavier by the valve stem would flop through the air. Air currents or wind may affect the flight of the serve, but only in one direction. Air currents do not bring about the spinless ball's dance.)

The harder a spinless ball is served, the more sharply it tends to jump. It does not need to be served hard, however, to fly in an unpredictable way. For this reason the spinless serve, often called a "floater," is the favorite at all levels of competition.

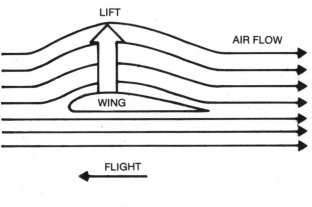

LIFT

AIR FLOW

WING

FLIGHT

69

70

71

72

There are two methods of serving a floater: the Asian (**71**) and the overhand serves (**72**). Allen Scates, in his book *Winning Volleyball*, writes: "The round-house [Asian] floater serve is currently the most effective for local, regional and national competition . . . ."* Why? The Asian is easier to do. First, the motion is simple: a body turn with the arm held nearly straight throughout (**71**). In contrast, the overhand serve requires the player to straighten his arm part by part (**72**). Second, the Asian serve gives greater power than the overhand. The player uses his whole body for the Asian, turning into the ball like a golfer or batter (**71**). He does not have to work as hard as the overhand server.

*Allen E. Scates, *Winning Volleyball*, Allyn and Bacon, Inc., 1976, page 15.

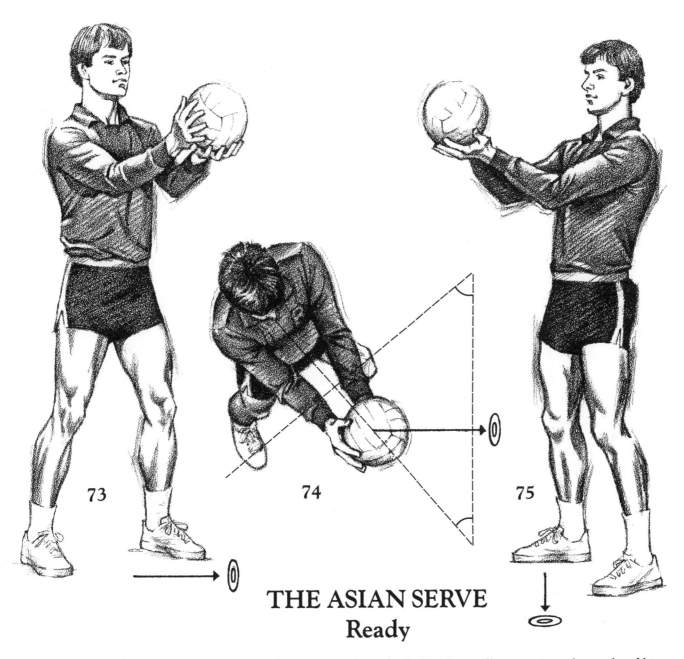

73

74

75

THE ASIAN SERVE
Ready

In the ready position, the Asian server's body is motionless and firm (**73**). His feet are flat on the floor, side-by-side and about shoulder width apart. He faces about 45 degrees to the right of the target (**74**).* His toes are at the same 45 degree angle. His weight is even. The player's knees are slightly bent, his back straight (**73, 75**).

The server locates the bottom of the ball directly in front of his breastbone (**73, 74, 75**). His left or lifting hand holds the ball from underneath. The server does not grip the ball. He cradles it, using the pads of his fingers for balance. His right hand rests lightly on the back of the ball (**73, 74**).**

The server's left elbow points down (**75**). It is bent, but not so bent that it touches his side. It rests a few inches in front of his body (**74**). This elbow position is important because it locates the ball the right distance from the server's body. From here he can lift the ball straight up. His right elbow, too, is comfortably bent (**73**). The server looks at the ball.

*Facing 45 degrees to the right of the target at ready allows the server to turn his body forward for contact. This means the greatest possible power. See page 83.

**Starting with the right hand on the ball helps the server to focus. It also helps in timing, since both hands can move from this position at once.

76a   b

The Coil

The Asian serve begins with three separate motions. The server's left hand
lifts the ball, his right hand draws back and his left foot moves forward (**a, b**).
These motions all start at once (they also end at once).

c

d

The Lift

The server lifts the ball with a smooth vertical motion (76). His hand stays in contact with the ball as long as possible, then releases it without spin (c). At the release, the server's arm is nearly straight. The ball rises from his hand about 6 inches only (d). Why so low? High throws are hard to hit squarely. They drop increasingly fast. And high throws turn small throwing mistakes into big ones. The ball must not be thrown lower than 6 inches, however. The server does not want to hurry the motion of his serving arm.

77a   b

The Right Hand

The server's right hand draws away from the ball at the start of the lift (**a, b**). His arm straightens as his hand reaches back (**c**).

His arm continues to move backward until it can go no further, stopped by his shoulder (**d**). His hand is now a few inches past the line of his hips. His shoulders rotate, too, until they, in turn, are stopped by his torso (**d**). His chest faces 90 degrees to the right of the target.

c   d

*Note that all of the server's weight has shifted to his right foot (**d**). He is coiled, ready to move into the ball.*

78a   b

The Step

The third motion is a light step with the left foot (**78**). The server's weight shifts to his right foot as his left moves forward (**a, b**). The step is short — 3 or 4 inches only — and in a line about 45 degrees to the left of the target (this is the same line set by his ready position — page 75, Fig. 74). The server has almost no weight on his left foot at the end of the movement; only his toe, pointing toward the target, touches the floor (**d**). The server's torso *does not* move forward with his left foot — he does not want to start his weight shift to his front foot too soon.

The server's body is coiled, ready to move into the ball (**d**). Both his serving arm and his right shoulder have rotated as far to the rear as possible. His weight has shifted to his back foot.

The player's serving hand has stopped about a foot in back of his right hip (**d**). It faces slightly back and is ready to contact the ball.

The server's elbow, wrist and hand are straight and firm. This does not change throughout the hit. His elbow can be a trouble spot. He does not want to "lock" it, to extend it all the way. To most servers, locking means that the arm is bent back, not straight. Also, it hurts to hit the ball with a fully extended elbow.

79a   b

The server's hand is ready to contact the ball (**79a**). It bends slightly where the fingers attach to the palm—at the big knuckles (**80**). The bend allows the player to hit the ball on the meat of his hand—both the heel and the edge. It also helps to stiffen the server's wrist, preventing waggle. Furthermore, the bend keeps the palm-side of his knuckles from sticking out and interfering with a clean hit. Each finger is straight; they are also spread (**79c**).

 *The server who tries to contact the ball with his arm more nearly vertical breaks the straight line made by his arm and shoulders. This means less power.

 **The server does not need to stop his hand to avoid spin. The ball springs quickly away. The path of his hand after contact has no effect on the flight of the serve.

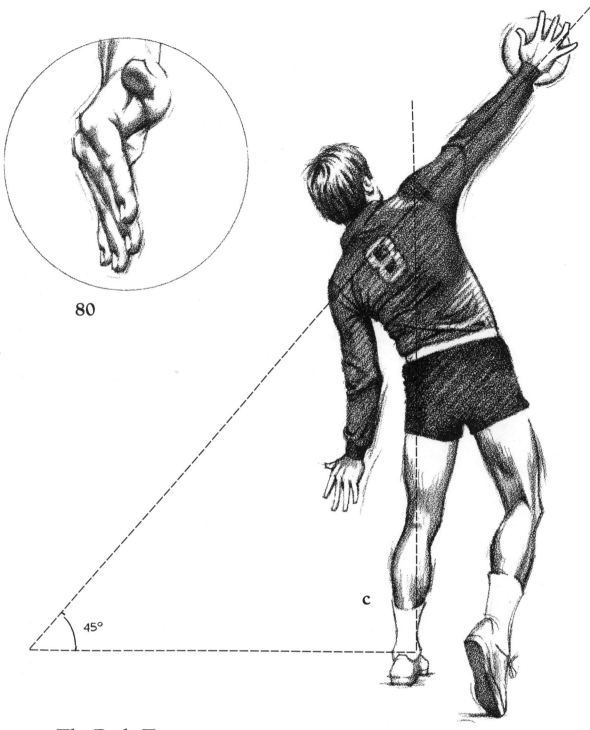

80

c

45°

The Body Turn

The server rotates his hips and shoulders into the ball (**79**). As his body turns, he shifts his weight from his back foot to his front one. The forceful turn of the server's body — accompanied by the weight shift — is the basis for the power of the Asian serve.

At contact, the server's body faces the target (**c**). His shoulders, arm and hand are in a line about 45 degrees to the floor.* His hand is moving fast.

The server contacts the exact center of the ball (**c**). His hand follows a line drawn through the ball's core (a diameter line). The slightest mistake puts spin on the ball.**

81a   b

The Weight Shift

The server's right hand rises, and his left hand drops as he moves into the ball (**81**). His shoulders reverse their angle, turning his arms like the vanes of a windmill (**a, d**).

The server's left foot — still pointing toward the target — steps firmly down at the beginning of his weight shift (**a, b**). As his weight moves forward, his front leg straightens (**b, c**).

c   d

At contact, the server's front leg has locked (**d**). All of his weight has moved to his front foot; only the toe of his back foot touches the floor. The left side of the server's body has stiffened. His leg, body and right arm make a vertical line (**d**). The server continues to watch the ball at contact.

*Note that the server's right shoulder leads his hand (**c**). This is important in whipping the ball, discussed on the next page.*

82a   b

The Whip

The server moves into the ball with a strong turn of his shoulders (82). Before contact, the line of his arm lags that of his shoulders by about a foot (measured at his hand) (a). When the server's shoulders are nearly facing the target, he slows their turn (b). His arm speeds up, acting like a whip. This whipping motion adds a great deal of power to the Asian serve. At contact, the server's shoulders and arm make a straight line, square to the target (b).

c

83

After contact, the server's arm continues to whip, crossing the line of his shoulders (c).

The server's arm has given up a great deal of its energy to the ball at contact. It sweeps — slowly — across his body as the ball speeds away (83). The player's left foot continues to carry all of his weight at the finish of the motion. His torso is locked against his left hip. The server is balanced, ready to take his position on the court.

84

85

I. In order to start his motion efficiently, the Asian server:

    1. Points his feet 45 degrees to the right of the target, shoulder width apart
    2. Distributes his weight evenly
    3. Cradles the ball in front of his breastbone
    4. Locates his left elbow a few inches in front of his body
    5. Looks at the ball

II. To "tee" the ball in the air, the server:

    1. Raises his left hand vertically
    2. Stays in contact with the ball as long as possible
    3. Allows the ball to rise from his hand about 6 inches only

III. To shift his weight into the ball, the server:

    1. Transfers all of his weight to his right foot
    2. Raises his left foot
    3. Moves his left foot slightly forward 45 degrees to the left of the target
    4. Touches his left toe lightly to the floor
    5. Points it toward the target

IV. To drive the ball with little effort, the server:

    1. Rotates his hips and shoulders into the ball
    2. Shifts his weight to his front foot
    3. Straightens his front leg
    4. Raises and whips his arm into the ball
    5. Drops his left arm

V. At contact, the server:

    1. Hits the exact center of the ball with the meat of his hand
    2. Faces directly toward the target
    3. Makes, with his serving arm and his shoulders, a line about 45 degrees to floor
    4. Locks his front leg

THE OVERHAND SERVE

86

The overhand serve is like the Asian in many ways. The timing—from beginning to end—is exactly the same. The lift of the ball is the same. So are the step and the weight shift. The hand and wrist position does not change from the Asian nor does the contact point of the ball. The biggest difference is in the bends at the elbow and shoulder (**86**). These mean more effort and, therefore, greater chance for error for the overhand server.

87

88

Ready

In the ready position, the server's body is solid. He faces about 45 degrees to the right of the target (**88**). His feet are flat on the floor and slightly wider than his shoulders. His right foot points in the same direction as his body — about 45 degrees to the right of the target (**88**). His left foot points slightly to the right of the target. He carries more weight on his right foot than his left (**87**). His knees are slightly bent, his back straight.

The server locates the ball directly in front of his right shoulder (**88**). He cradles the ball in his left hand at shoulder height (**87**). His right hand rests on the back of the ball, helping him to focus. His left arm is comfortably bent. The server looks at the ball.

89

The Coil

Like the Asian serve, the overhand begins with three separate motions. The server's left hand lifts the ball, his right arm draws back and his left foot moves forward (89). These motions all start at once and also end at once.

90a   b

The Lift

The overhand server lifts the ball with a smooth vertical motion, just like the Asian server (**a, b**). His hand stays in contact with the ball as long as possible, then releases it without spin (**c**). The ball rises from his hand less than a foot — once again just like the Asian.

c   d

The Right Hand

    The server's right hand draws away from the ball at the start of the lift (**a, b**). His elbow remains high as it leads his arm back. His arm continues to move until it is stopped by his shoulder (**c, d**). Both his upper arm and his forearm are nearly in line with the target. His palm turns slightly outward.

91a   b

The server draws his elbow as far to the rear as possible (**a, b, c**). The player's right forearm angles slightly upward toward the ball at the end of his drawback (**c**). His arm is now coiled, ready to unfold like a whip.

The server arches his back *very little* during the drawback of his arm. A large arching movement interferes with both the vertical lift of the ball and a complete drawback of the player's elbow.

c

d

The Step

The server takes a light step forward during his lift of the ball (**91**). As he steps, his weight shifts to his right foot (**a, b**). The step is about a foot long and directly toward the target. His left leg is slightly bent when his foot touches down (**d**). His torso moves forward only slightly with the step.

The Hit

The Body Turn

The server begins to rotate his hips and shoulders into the ball (**a, b**).
His right shoulder, just like the spiker's, leads the way. His left arm moves
downward and his right hand sweeps back.

c

d

The server's elbow rises toward the ball during his body turn (**c**). Like the spiker's, his elbow does not move ahead of the line of his shoulders. He does not want to uncoil his arm before he has finished his shoulder turn.

At contact, the server's body faces the target (**d**). His arm is bent (unlike the spiker's). A bent arm allows greater firmness at the shoulder and more control. His hand is held as if it were Asian serving—with a slight bend at the big knuckles (page 83, Fig. 80). He contacts the exact center of the ball; his wrist is firm.

93a   b

The Weight Shift

As the server moves into the ball, his weight shifts from his back to his front foot (**93**). His front leg straightens; his body becomes increasingly firm.

His elbow rises toward the ball (**a, b, c**). When his elbow is in line with his ear, his arm begins to straighten (**c**).

c   d

At contact, the server's left leg carries all his weight; it is firm (**d**). His shoulders are square to the target. His forearm is vertical, with a slight bend at the elbow.

94a   b   c

The Whip

The overhand server drives his elbow toward the ball (**a**). His elbow slows, allowing his forearm to speed up (**b**). His forearm continues to speed up until contact. His arm does not straighten entirely — completing its whip — until the ball is on its way (**c**). By this time his arm is going slowly. Its motion has been transferred to the ball.

95

At the finish of his motion, the server carries his entire weight on his left foot; his right toe rests lightly on the floor. His right hand has followed the ball forward so that his arm angles downward. The server is perfectly balanced.

96

97

4-47

98a   b

THE TOPSPIN SERVE

The spinner is a very effective serve when it goes into the court (**98**). The server simply overpowers his opposition; even when the ball is contacted solidly by the passer, it sometimes spins away. Use of the spin serve has increased in recent years, particularly in combination with a jump.

The spin server must bend his back deeply for power (**a**). This takes time and means that he must lift the ball very high. The ball rises about 3 feet from his hand (**a**). As in serving the floater, the player transfers all of his weight onto his front foot as he contacts the ball (**b**). His left side— leg, hip and torso—is firm. Unlike in serving the floater, his arm is straight at contact (**b**). It is also vertical. As in spiking, the server snaps his wrist over the ball, giving it topspin. The server finishes his motion with balance.

99a   b

THE JUMP SERVE

The jump serve is a variation of the spinner (**99**). The server jumps well into his own court before contact. He is closer to and higher above his opponents than the conventional server. This means a larger target. However, the jump server, who uses a very high lift of the ball and a powerful jump, has a great chance of making an error.

The server uses the same four-step approach as in spiking. This includes a full armswing. He measures his steps so that he jumps near the baseline.

The server cradles the ball in both hands as he starts forward (**a**). He lifts it high and in front of him on his second step (his left foot). Now he continues as if he were spiking. There is one difference: he jumps as far forward as possible, landing well inside his own court (**b**).

I. In the ready position, the overhand server:

    1. Faces 45 degrees to the right of the target
    2. Positions his feet flat on the floor
    3. Puts more weight on his back foot than his front
    4. Holds the ball in front of his right shoulder

II. At the start of the motion, the server:

    1. Lifts the ball straight up
    2. Draws back his right elbow
    3. Steps forward with his left foot

III. The server must remember, above all to:

    1. Draw back his right elbow as far and as high as possible
    2. Drive his right shoulder forward
    3. To keep his elbow in line with—not ahead of—his shoulder turn
    4. Press his left foot firmly down at contact
    5. Bend his right elbow slightly at contact

CHAPTER V
THE BLOCK

The block is a method of driving an attacked ball back into the opponents' court (100). It takes place next to the net and is volleyball's first line of defense. The blocking motion is simple and, compared to the spike, effortless. It gains strong results from staying, that is, from holding its position. The blocker's hands remain over the net—stuffing the ball—after the spiker's hand has gone. The most powerful block stems from a powerful spike.

100

101

Ready

The blocker positions his feet side-by-side, the width of his shoulders or wider (**101**). They are flat on the floor with his weight on the front part. He holds his hands comfortably above his shoulders, palms forward. He spreads his fingers and bends his knees slightly. His back is straight. He watches his opponents' attack as it develops.

The Block

When the player has decided it is the time and place to block, he quickly lowers his weight (**a**). His hips move backward; his back is straight. When his knees are near a right angle, he pauses, ready to jump. His face remains vertical; he does not look down or change the angle of his head.

The blocker jumps vertically (**b**). His arms straighten, firming from shoulder to fingertip. His thumbs angle up; a distance of less than 8 inches between them (the diameter of the ball) keeps the ball from going through.

102a

b

c

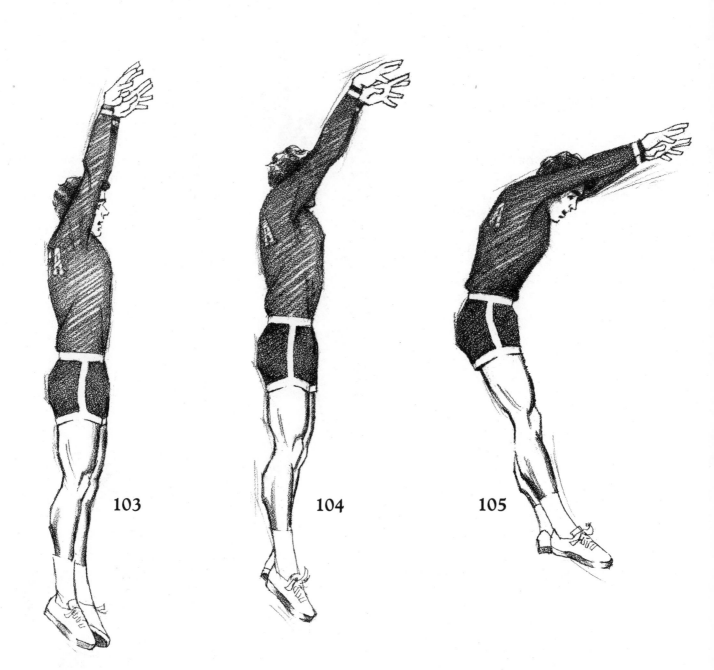

103

104

105

1. If the blocker cannot jump so that his wrists are above the net, his body stays vertical at the height of his jump. His hands and arms reach forward only enough to close the gap between his hands and the net.

2. If he can reach his wrists above the net, he presses his hands forward at the height of his jump (**103**). This allows him to contact the ball slightly sooner and to push it downward.

3. If the blocker can reach any part of his forearms or his elbows above the net, he presses his arms forward (**104**). This allows him to reach across the net and touch the ball soon after the spiker has hit it.

4. If he can reach his shoulders above the net, he presses forward at the waist (**105**). This allows him to reach deep into his opponents' court, pushing the ball down as it is being spiked.

106a   b   c

Getting to the Ball

The Side-Step

Side-stepping is the easiest and most controlled way to move to the ball (**106**). The blocker faces his opponents throughout the movement. Outside blockers almost always use the side-step to adjust their position.

Cross-Over Step

Side-steps are too short for the middle blocker, who must quickly travel 10 feet or more. He needs a cross-over step. He leads with the foot nearer the blocking site and follows with his cross-over (**a, b**).

107a   b

The blocker turns his right foot toward the net as he arrives in his blocking position (**c**). This allows him to complete his turn easily (**d**). He jumps facing the net (**e**). His hands remain in front of his body, ready to reach and press, throughout his movement to the ball.

c

d

e

The Spike Approach

Stopping and turning toward the net before the jump brings control. But it also keeps the blocker from using all of his forward motion to gain a higher jump. For this reason shorter middle blockers (and some outside blockers) use a spike approach. The blocker once again starts with a short step (**a**). This time he follows with a long running step and a spike armswing, keeping his side to the net (**b, c**).

108a

b

The blocker does not face the net when he jumps; rather, he angles his side toward it (**d**). He turns slowly in the air, facing his opponents at the top of his jump (**e**).

Most of the time the three steps of the spike approach bring the player into blocking position. If he must cover more distance, he adds an even number of steps to his approach: two, four or more.

c

d

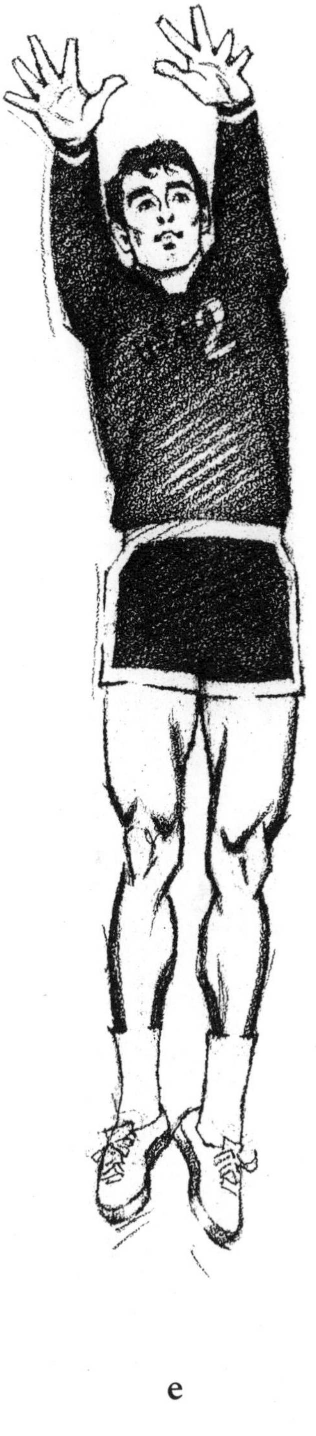

e

109

CHAPTER VI

THE BACKCOURT

110

The backcourt player must control an attacked ball that has passed his team's block. He is the last line of defense and can often save a rally. There are four defensive techniques that make his job easier. The dig allows the player to receive a hard spike. The roll, dive and collapse allow him to throw himself onto the floor to retrieve the ball. A spectacular save in the backcourt, more than any other play, can inspire a team (**110**).

111

THE DIG

The dig is a method of receiving a hard spike, usually with the forearms (**111**). The term originated, according to legend, from beach volleyball. Saving a ball meant "digging" into the sand. A dig can be made with one or both forearms.

112

113

Moving

The backcourt player wants to position himself where he thinks the ball will arrive. As his opponents' attack unfolds, he is in constant motion, trying to find just the right spot to receive the ball. He moves forward, back, left or right. He takes small steps, large ones or runs at full speed.

When his opponents attack only with soft shots, the backcourt player can keep his body high and relaxed as he moves (112). This allows him to move his feet quickly to the ball, as in receiving serve. He can cover a large section of court and still arrive under control. He is also in a good position to re-

ceive a high, off-speed shot with an overhand pass.

When his opponents hit the ball hard, the backcourt player must coil his body and spring for the ball. Springing is very quick, but less controlled than receiving the ball in a high, relaxed position. To be ready to spring, the player must lower his body during his movement (113).

A low body position not only coils the player's body for the spring but shortens his distance to the floor. This makes it easier to receive spikes hit low. The defender can still spring upward to dig a high attack.

114a   b

The Hop

The defender has lowered his body and adjusted his location on the court. He faces the attack. Now he makes one more move to obtain the greatest chance to dig a hard spike. He makes a short hop toward the attack (a, b). The hop helps the digger to spring or explode toward a hard hit. But it also leaves him in good position to make the other moves required to defend his area: to collapse, dive or roll.*

When the defender guards against a multiple attack, he does not know when or from what direction the spike will come. In this case he must make a hop for each possible spike, meaning a series of hops during one attack.

*The collapse, dive and roll are discussed separately from the dig. Their emphasis is in throwing oneself to the floor without pain. The emphasis in the dig is in receiving the ball, particularly when the player can stay on his feet.

c

d

The hopper lands slightly before the ball is hit (**c**). His feet are side-by-side and wider than his shoulders. His body is at its most coiled upon landing. Now he begins to uncoil (**d**). He moves his weight upward and slightly forward. He rises slowly. He has not yet started to spring, but his legs are already pushing him toward the attack. He has forward momentum.

115

116

The Spring

At the instant the defender sees the at-tack, he makes his spring.* He can move in any direction. When he has positioned him-self in the ball's path, the defender pushes up-ward and receives it on both forearms (115). He draws his arms toward his body. They are nearly vertical; this prevents the spiked ball—arriving with hard topspin—from jumping backward. The player thrusts his hips forward for balance as he moves upward. He does not need to clasp his hands. He does, however, press the heels of his hands to-gether so that his arms are square.

*Occasionally the defender will not need to spring. He will have guessed perfectly the path of the attack. In this case he only needs to straighten his body and bring his forearms together. He remains still and balanced throughout his move.

117

118

When the ball has been hit outside the midline of his body, the defender would like to move in front of it (116). This allows him to see the ball well and to keep his arms square and still. But on the hardest hits, the digger does not have time to move in front of the ball. He must pivot quickly on the foot furthest from the ball as he spins his shoulders (117). This brings his arms swinging toward the path of the ball.

The player tries to keep his arms together during their swing. This gives him a controlled, two-arm contact of the ball (117). But when the ball is hit very hard, or is almost out of reach, the player's arms may split (118). The defender has less control with split arms but can move his leading arm more quickly. The digger wants to face his forearms as much as possible toward the front.

119

When the ball is hit a distance from the digger, he must take a short step toward it (**119**). He does not have time to receive the ball with both arms. He must spring with one arm extended, hoping to deflect the ball upward so that a teammate can help.

120

121

Emergencies

When the ball is hit near the defender's face, he must bring his hands up to protect himself. He can dig the ball with his hands up, but the contact must be very clean to avoid a foul. The quickest way is to use an open hand (**120**). The defender holds his hand palm-up. This deflects the ball upward.

Sometimes the player will have time to raise both hands (**121**). In this case he can clasp them by cupping one over the other. Contact is made on the edges of both hands. Two-handed contact is firmer than one-handed, resulting in greater control and fewer fouls.

122

Receiving the Off-Speed Attack

Not all attacks that intend to result in a hard spike do so. When the defender has determined that the ball will not be hit hard, he rises from his low posture (**122**). This allows him once again to move his feet quickly, covering a large section of the court with control. Raising his hands puts him in position to receive a high ball with an overhand pass.

123

124

Special Contacts

When the defender is chasing a ball off the court, he must pass the ball over his shoulder. He angles his hands backward by curling or "jaying" his wrists at contact (**123**). He must also "jay" his wrists when he is chasing a ball toward the net or when he needs to get up a ball that has been hit at a steep angle.

When the ball is low and almost out of reach, the digger can use the "pancake." He flattens his hand firmly on the floor, allowing the ball to bounce from it (**124**).

The Range of the Dig

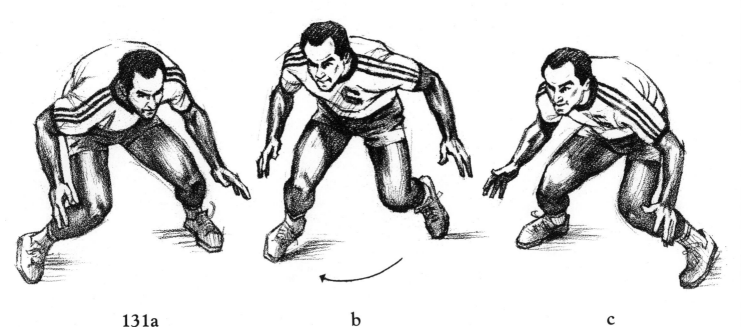

131a   b   c

The defender continues to cover the court even after he sees that the
ball has been hit away from him. Now he must play rebounds from his teammates.

The defender has hopped into digging position, facing the attack (**a**). The
ball is hit past him, for example, on his right. He has one more hop to make: a
spinner toward the arrival site of the ball (**b**). The defender keeps his body low
throughout his hop, landing in digging position (**c**). He is ready to receive a ball
driven toward him or to run for a ball deflected off the court.

132

THE DIVE

All floor skills—the dive, the roll and the collapse—allow the defender to stretch his body horizontally without hurting himself. The dive differs from the other two in that it starts with a powerful jump—the diver flies through the air (132). The dive requires the upper body strength to do a push-up or two and is the most tiring floor skill. Men usually prefer to dive rather than to roll.

133a

b

The player runs toward the ball (**a**). The right-hander would like to take off with his left foot (**b**). This allows him to reach farther with his right hand. He lowers his body on the last step; he also draws back his arms in readiness for their drive toward the ball (**b**).

134

c

As he pushes off, he kicks his rear foot into the air, bringing his body horizontal (c). His back is arched, his head up. When he needs to play the ball forward or up, he makes contact with the back of one hand (c). If the ball is not too far away, he may clasp his hands and contact the ball on both forearms. This brings greater control. If he needs to hit the ball sideways or back over his shoulder, he uses his thumb and index finger together (134).

135a   b

The player's hands touch the floor (**a**). He continues to keep his head and feet up; his body forms a letter "C." He pushes with his arms, lowering his body gently to the floor. His chest touches first, followed by his stomach and then his hips. His hands push to the rear, helping him to slide (**b**). Now the diver must bring himself quickly to his feet in order to continue play.

The player can dive directly from the ready-to-dig position as well as from a run. In this case the dive acts as a recovery from a spring. (The full dive sequence is shown on pages 142 and 143.)

136

THE ROLL

The roll is the only method of "going to the floor" that brings the player back to her feet (136). The player's use of her momentum does the trick. She does not resist her momentum as in diving or collapsing. She simply guides it. This makes the roll the least tiring of the three floor skills. Women more often roll than dive.

137a   **b**

To retrieve a ball to her left, the player takes a short step toward the ball with her left foot (**a**). This starts her momentum. After a skip step, she takes a long step toward the ball (**b**).* She draws back her contact hand in readiness for its reach for the ball. Her opposite hand is held out for balance (**b**).

*She does not need a skip step when she is already running toward the ball.

c

The roller falls toward the ball (**c**). She allows her weight to move over and past her front foot. Her leading knee turns inward to avoid hitting the floor. She reaches toward the ball, contacting it with the heel, the back, or the thumb and index finger of her left hand.

138a   b

After the touch, the player slides the heel of her hand lightly along the floor, easing her body down (**a**). Her side—from her hip to her hand—touches the floor (**b**). Both knees are bent. She rolls on a diagonal line across her body—from her left hip to her right shoulder (**a, b**). Her right arm stays near her side on the floor, with her hand held palm up. This is important. If her arm or hand strays, it can resist her momentum.

c

d

The player's right knee leads her body over; the toe of her right foot touches the floor (**c**). Her left foot follows, still on the diagonal line. Her left arm helps to support her as she returns to her feet (**c**). She finishes with balance, ready for the next play (**d**).

139

140

142

141

The roller is not restricted to movement to the side. She can roll in any direction that she can step, including directly to the front (**141**).

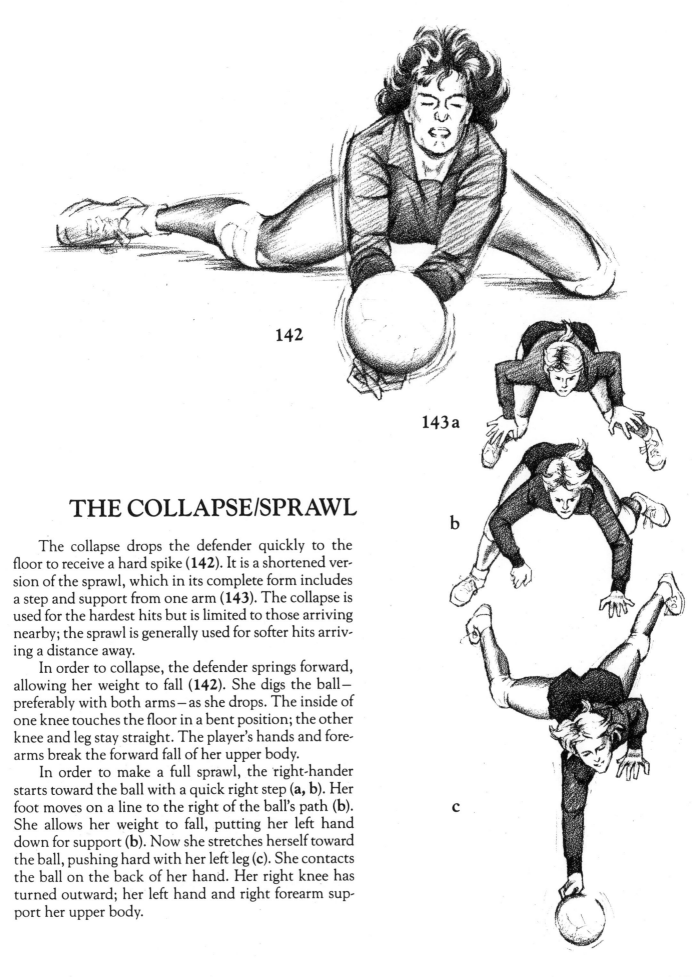

142

143 a

b

c

THE COLLAPSE/SPRAWL

The collapse drops the defender quickly to the floor to receive a hard spike (**142**). It is a shortened version of the sprawl, which in its complete form includes a step and support from one arm (**143**). The collapse is used for the hardest hits but is limited to those arriving nearby; the sprawl is generally used for softer hits arriving a distance away.

In order to collapse, the defender springs forward, allowing her weight to fall (**142**). She digs the ball—preferably with both arms—as she drops. The inside of one knee touches the floor in a bent position; the other knee and leg stay straight. The player's hands and forearms break the forward fall of her upper body.

In order to make a full sprawl, the right-hander starts toward the ball with a quick right step (**a, b**). Her foot moves on a line to the right of the ball's path (**b**). She allows her weight to fall, putting her left hand down for support (**b**). Now she stretches herself toward the ball, pushing hard with her left leg (**c**). She contacts the ball on the back of her hand. Her right knee has turned outward; her left hand and right forearm support her upper body.

The Range of the Collapse

* * * * *

The distinctions among the floor skills—dive, roll and collapse—are becoming more and more blurred. Present-day players combine the use of all three. The sprawl is shortened to the collapse, as mentioned. The roll becomes a slide when the defender does not somersault; support from one hand adds a part of the sprawl. By far the most widely used combination involves the dive and the sprawl. The defender jumps toward the ball as in diving but touches down one hand, one forearm, one knee or a combination of all three.

CHAPTER VII
OTHER
ATTACKS

151

The spike, volleyball's most powerful shot, is the preferred attack by any player who can do it. But other attacks are useful, too. The floor spike is an easy attack for the beginning player. The dump drops a ball into the opponents' court on the second touch. The tip and chip shots each trick opponents who are expecting a hard spike. The wipe-off gives the attacker an alternative to being blocked (**151**).

152

THE FLOOR SPIKE

The floor spike is a method of hitting the ball into the opponents' court without a jump (**152**). It is like the overhand serve in all ways but two: the floor spiker must adjust her location before the hit, and she usually hits the ball with topspin (Chapter IV).

153a   b   c

Getting to the Ball

The right-handed attacker positions her feet in stride by stepping forward with her left foot (a). She points her left hand toward the ball and draws back her right elbow.

The spiker moves to the hitting spot with a series of left steps followed by skips (a, b). This allows her to arrive at the hitting spot with her left foot leading (c). The spiker bends her knees as she moves to the ball; she keeps her arms ready to hit throughout.

154a   **b**

The Hit

The spiker's right elbow is high at ready (**a**). At the start of the hit, she moves her hips and her weight forward (**b**). Her front foot is flat on the floor. Her hitting arm moves exactly as it would for the overhand serve or the spike (page 59).

154c

d

The spiker's shoulder and elbow drive toward the ball (c). Most of her weight has now moved onto her front foot.

The spiker hits with a controlled wrist snap, putting topspin on the ball. All of her weight is on her front foot at contact; her hitting arm is bent for greater control.

155

The Finish

After the hit, the spiker's arm continues to move slowly toward the target (**155**). She finishes her motion with all her weight carried on her left leg, which is straight. She is balanced, ready for the next play.

156   157

THE TIP

    The tip or dink is a soft, fingertip push of the ball from a spike approach (**156, 157**). It is intended to surprise a defense that expects a hard- driven spike. The tip is the easiest shot in volleyball.

    The approach for the tip is like the spike approach in every way (Chapter III). At the peak of the attacker's jump, she reaches as high as possible and touches the ball with all five fingers (**156**). She pushes the ball softly, using her entire arm. Her wrist and elbow move very little.

THE DUMP

The dump is a surprise tip by the setter (**158**). Since it takes place on the second instead of the third touch, it greatly changes the rhythm of a team's offense. The dump often catches the opponents off guard.

The setter jumps exactly as if she were going to make a set (**158**). She wants the ball to fall toward her forehead, as usual. She holds her hands in setting position. As the ball nears her hands, she quickly raises her left hand, turning its palm toward her opponents. She touches the side—not the bottom—of the ball; the pads of her fingers make contact. A smooth wrist flip drives the ball over the net (**158**). Her right hand does not change its position throughout the tip.

The setter wants to disguise her intentions as much as possible. Jumping whenever she is near the net helps her to confuse her opponents. Jumping even creates doubt when the setter has rotated to the back row (from which rotation she cannot legally attack a ball above the net).

158

THE CHIP

The chip or spin-dink is a short attack shot that spins from the spiker's palm (**159**). It is harder to control than the tip, but it happens fast and looks like a spike. It is the spiker's most deceptive shot.

The approach for the chip is exactly like that for the spike. The player jumps high, arches her back and pulls her right elbow back as far as possible (**a**). From this position she raises her hand straight up from her shoulder (**b**). Her hand is rounded like the ball.

159a

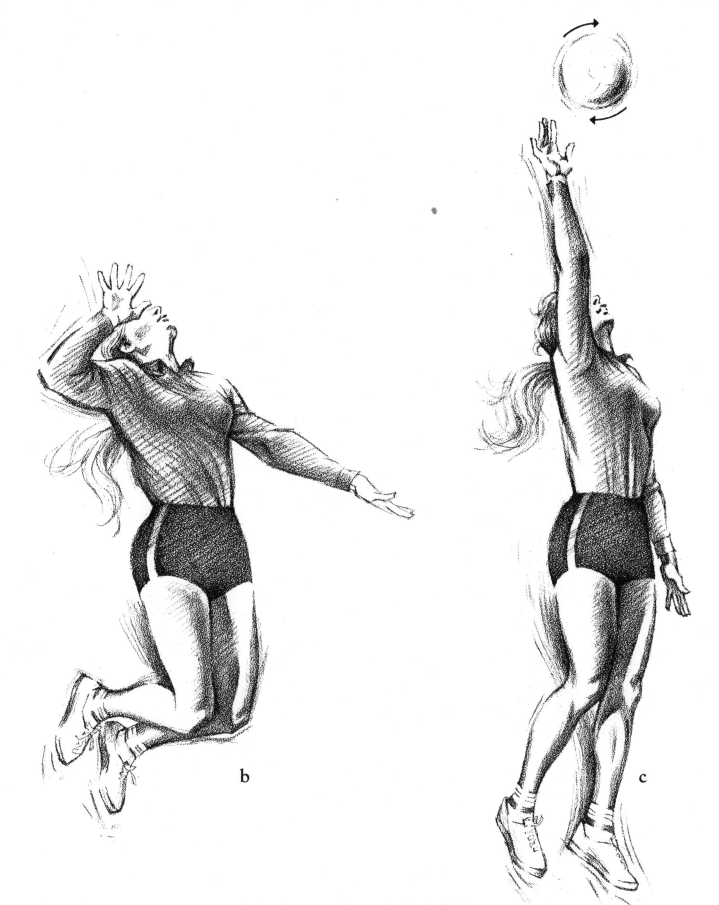

b

c

The player makes contact behind, not underneath the ball; she gets only a "piece" of it (**c**). This means that she can move her arm quickly upward but send the ball a short distance only. Her entire hand touches the ball: palm, fingers and thumb. Her arm continues to straighten and finally stops at full extension (**c**).

161a

THE WIPE-OFF

The wipe-off uses the blocker's hands. When the ball is set close to the net, the blocker has the advantage. She can reach over the net and smother the attack. But a smart attacker pushes the ball into the blocker's hands and out-of-bounds (**161**).

The attacker uses a spike approach and jump. Her reach for the ball can be compared to the tip: she uses all five fingers to touch the ball; she contacts it as high as possible (**a**). High contact gives the blocker less chance to push the ball down.

The attacker directs the ball toward the blocker's hand nearer the sideline (**a**). She pushes the ball firmly, keeping her hand on the ball. At the touch by the blocker, the attacker turns her hand and sweeps the ball out-of-bounds (**b**). She must be careful to withdraw her hand quickly to avoid touching the net.

EPILOGUE

The idea of "perfect technique" is anathema to some. Teams that have been strongly taught and that perform the skills similarly are considered mechanical and lacking in spontaneity. Players should be allowed to develop their own ways—what is most natural—according to this school of thought. There is no such thing as "perfect technique."

The problem stems from volleyball's newness. The sport is still rapidly evolving, particularly at the lower levels of play. The forearm pass, for example, is only about 25 years old. Other skills, notably the chip and the collapse, are younger still.

In contrast is the game of golf. Historical records show that people were playing the game before the time of Columbus, meaning that the golf swing is over 500 years old. By the middle of the 20th century (and perhaps considerably earlier), the best golfers had gained a clear idea of how to swing a golf club: they gripped the club by pressing their palms together, kept their left arms straight on the backswing, rotated their hips into the ball and shifted their weight from back foot to front foot. In 1957 these ideas were disseminated in a book entitled *The Modern Fundamentals of Golf* by Ben Hogan. From that point on, golfers at all levels of play could understand what had previously been known by only the few: the elements of the perfect swing.

Volleyball skills can be compared to the golf swing in mid-century: the best players in the world have a clear idea of how to do them. Their bodies, through repetition, have simply *found* the most effective ways. Thus, forearm passers at the international level hold their heads still and their feet side-by-side; international setters position their hands wide in order to squeeze the ball; spikers finish with their bodies straight (except when they are off balance or desperate). Asian serves are common, particularly among the women.

Unfortunately, the techniques shared by the best players in the world are not common among the many. Club and school players still straighten their legs in forearm passing; a commanding arm squeeze on the set is rare; few amateurs are able to hit without a pike. The biggest omission is the Asian serve: there is only one team in the USA that uses it exclusively—and with dominating success. This book was written with the idea of giving all volleyball players the knowledge advanced by the best players in the world.

APPENDIX

Appendix to Chapter I

A child has little ability to see an object and move herself or her hands to it. Throw her a ball and it bounces from her chest before she can catch it. The ball simply moves too fast for her to see.

The inexperienced passer has a similar problem. Although she can see the ball, she has trouble judging its location. She cannot tell whether the ball has been served high or low, left or right until it is near. She moves late.

The inexperienced passer's problem is not an inability to move or a lack of being ready, but of judging the location of the ball. And yet coaches often respond to this inability to judge by teaching their players to move—usually their feet—at ready. This is a mistake. Any movement other than a slight swaying for balance increases the player's reaction time by interfering with her vision. The inexperienced passer needs to watch more serves, not dance at ready.

* * * * *

Individual player movement is nearly sacred to some volleyball coaches. To them a moving body or a moving player is always better than one that is still. This applies to the pass: a position that is solid or stable cannot be good. There are, however, many examples in sports that show that quieting the head and the body can be beneficial—especially in hand/eye movements.

The sacrifice bunter in softball wants, above all, to contact the ball squarely. She turns to face the pitcher and holds her head and body very still as she watches the ball. Her vision is sharp. During the bunt, she needs only to move her bat and is usually successful in making contact. In contrast, the drag bunter wants not only to contact the ball but also to reach first base before the throw. She is moving, starting her run to first as she tries to bunt. She often misses the ball entirely.

The receiver in football is more likely to catch the ball when he is standing still than when he is on the run. Standing still in a pass pattern is not deceptive but, like the sacrifice bunt, sure. Moreover, the receiver, like the forearm passer, can still spring for the ball if needed. Being still allows him to move quickly in any direction.

Finally, the baseball outfielder does not try to time his run to a fly ball so that he and the ball arrive at the catching site at the same time. Instead, he runs very fast to the catching site, adjusts his position and catches the ball standing nearly still.

Stillness* simply allows the player to know exactly where she is in relation to everything else. All of the environment serves as a reference. Her vision is at its best.

* * * * *

Ready positions are often stylized in ways that work against quick movement. Extending the arms toward the server brings an air of determination to the receiver at ready. However, she must bring her arms back toward her body before she can move. Extending the arms means an extra, unnecessary motion.

---

*"Still" must not be confused with "tight" or "tense." "Still" is not inhibiting.

Appendix to Chapter III

"The harder the spiker hits the ball, the more his body stops at contact." This seems contrary. We would expect the hitter's hand to follow through more quickly or completely on the hardest hits. But both the spiker and the ball are in midair. Contact between them must be seen as a collision between two bodies, each of which has no support.

The easiest way to understand the results of the collision is by making a comparison. Consider a falcon colliding with a volleyball. The falcon would not sustain much impact if it were flying at 5 mph when it hit the ball. But if its speed were increased to 100 mph, it would sustain a great impact. Its speed would decrease drastically at contact. The spiker's hand and body work the same way. The harder the spiker's hand collides with the ball, the greater the impact for the spiker. The more drastically his hand and body slow at contact.

* * * * *

"The spiker develops his greatest power when his body has returned to perfectly straight." The easiest way to consider this idea is once again by making a comparison.

Imagine a flexible rod suspended vertically by four cables. The cables are tight, holding the rod at the midpoint of its length. Now the top and bottom of the rod are drawn back like a bow is bent in archery. Both the top and bottom move an equal distance in the same direction.

The bent rod wants to return to its starting position, to straighten. In the language of physics, it has "restoring force" when it is bent. Now both the top and bottom of the rod are released. The rod straightens. Its speed of straightening increases as it moves closer and closer to its starting position. The rod is moving at its fastest when it is once again perfectly straight. In the language of physics, it has "maximum velocity" at this point.

Since the rod is flexible, it does not stop when it has returned to straight. It bends in the opposite direction. The rod's speed of bending in the new direction begins to decrease the moment it passes perfectly straight. Its speed continues to decrease until it stops, ready to straighten again in the opposite direction.

The spiker can be compared to the rod held by cables. He is suspended in midair; he bends his body to make a "C"; he straightens for power. But the most important comparison concerns speed: the tips of the spiker's body, like the tips of the rod, are moving at their fastest when they return to perfectly straight. One of these "tips" is the spiker's hitting hand.

BIBLIOGRAPHY

Bertucci, Bob, *Championship Volleyball (by the Experts)*, Leisure Press, West Point, NY, 1979.

Coleman, James E., & Taras N. Liskevych, *Pictorial Analysis of Power Volleyball*, Creative Sports Books, Carmichael, CA, 1976.

Dunphy, Marv, *Volleyball*, Grosset and Dunlap, New York, 1980.

Hare, Dennis (with Jill Esteras), *The Art of Beach Volleyball*, Hogar Publishing Co., San Bernardino, CA, 1981.

Herzog, Karl, *Volleyball, Movements in Photographic Sequence*, Team-L Volleyball, Dulman, Federal Republic of Germany, 1975.

Jerome, John, *The Sweet Spot in Time*, Summit Books, New York, 1980.

Keller, Val, *Point, Game, and Match*, Creative Sports Books, Hollywood, CA, 1968.

Matsudaira, Yasutaka, Naohiro Ikeda, & Masaru Saito, *Winning Volleyball*, Canadian Volleyball Association, Vanier, Ontario, Canada, 1977.

Morehouse, Laurence E., & Leonard Gross, *Maximum Performance*, Pocket Books, New York, 1977.

Prsala, Jan, & Jim Hoyle, *Volleyball for Everybody*, Dalhousie University, Halifax, Nova Scotia, Canada, 1982.

Scates, Allen E., *Winning Volleyball*, Allyn & Bacon, Boston, MA, 1976.

Schaafsma, Frances, & Ann Heck, *Volleyball for Coaches and Teachers*, Wm. C. Brown Co., Dubuque, IA, 1971.

INDEX

About the Author

Jeff Lucas has played in well over 100 U.S. Volleyball Association tournaments in the past 15 years, including three National Championships in the 35-and-over division. One of his National tournament teams included U.S. Olympic gold medal winning coaches Doug Beal and Bill Neville.

Lucas has coached volleyball for 10 years. In eight years of coaching at Wenatchee, Washington, High School, his teams played in the AAA State Tournament five times, finishing fourth and third before winning the championship in 1983. He received second degree coaching certification—the highest available—from the International Volleyball Federation in 1980. Lucas has a B.A. in history from Stanford (1968) and did graduate work in business at Columbia.

About the Artist

Portrait artist Stuart Moldrem paints oil portraits and teaches fine art at the Moldrem Atelier School of Art in Seattle, Washington. Mr. Moldrem is listed in *Who's Who in American Art*. For 35 years he had a drama and sports feature in the *Seattle Post-Intelligencer*. In the U.S. Army he was the only artist on the staff of the *Stars & Stripes* newspaper. He received international recognition in 1967 by the *Salon Internationale de la Caricature* for achievement in journalistic art. Mr. Moldrem was cited for "Excellence in Journalism" by Sigma Delta Chi in 1965, '66, '74, '75 and twice in 1977. Stuart Moldrem is a tournament tennis player and now a volleyball fan.